The Milkshake Book

30 of the CREAMIEST and Delicious Milkshakes Ever!

BY

Stephanie Sharp

Copyright © 2019 by Stephanie Sharp

License Notes

Copyright 2019 by Stephanie Sharp All rights reserved.

No part of this Book may be transmitted or reproduced into any format for any means without the proper permission of the Author. This includes electronic or mechanical methods, photocopying or printing.

The Reader assumes all risk when following any of the guidelines or ideas written as they are purely suggestion and for informational purposes. The Author has taken every precaution to ensure accuracy of the work but bears no responsibility if damages occur due to a misinterpretation of suggestions.

My deepest thanks for buying my book! Now that you have made this investment in time and money, you are now eligible for free e-books on a weekly basis! Once you subscribe by filling in the box below with your email address, you will start to receive free and discounted book offers for unique and informative books. There is nothing more to do! A reminder email will be sent to you a few days before the promotion expires so you will never have to worry about missing out on this amazing deal. Enter your email address below to get started. Thanks again for your purchase!

Just visit the link or scan QR-code to get started!

https://stephanie-sharp.subscribemenow.com

Table of Contents

Introduction 8

Classic Vanilla Milkshake 10

Cookie Dough Milkshake 12

Oreo Milkshake with Chocolate Ganache 15

Apple and Cinnamon Milkshake 18

Coffee Milkshake 20

Banana Milkshake 23

Chocolate Peanut Butter Milkshake 25

Cinnamon Roll Milkshakes 27

Classic Chocolate Milkshake 29

Pumpkin Spice Milkshake 32

Vanilla Chai Milkshake 34

Strawberry Milkshake 36

Pina Colada Milkshake... 38

Nutella Milkshake 40

Salted Caramel Milkshake 42

Blueberry Milkshake 45

Biscoff Milkshake 47

Key Lime Pie Milkshakes 49

KitKat Milkshake 51

Mango and Passionfruit Milkshake................................. 53

White Chocolate Mocha Milkshake................................ 55

Matcha Green Tea Milkshake 58

Cannoli Milkshake 60

Coconut Almond Milkshake 62

Red Velvet Milkshake 64

Tiramisu Milkshakes 66

White Chocolate Raspberry Milkshake 68

Dark Chocolate Brownie Milkshake 71

Peach Pie Milkshake 74

Cotton Candy Milkshake 76

Conclusion 78

About the Author 79

Author's Afterthoughts 80

Introduction

Looking for a quick and delicious dessert that takes minimal effort? How about a rich and creamy milkshake? If your answers to both those questions was a yes (of course it was), then this book is for you! You'll find 30 of the most delicious and drool-worth milkshake recipes that take less than 15 minutes to make.

Almost every recipe uses just a few numbers of ingredients that come together to create some of the best milkshakes you've ever had. Cold, creamy and decadent are simple words that don't do these milkshakes justice. So just grab your blender and let's get started!

Classic Vanilla Milkshake

Creamy, rich and delicious, this classic vanilla milkshake is out-of-this-world good!

Makes: 6 servings

Prep: 10 mins

Ingredients:

- 4 1/2 cups vanilla ice cream
- 3 cups whole milk
- 1 ½ tsp vanilla extract
- Whipped cream, for topping
- Cherries, for topping

Directions:

1. Place the vanilla ice cream, milk and vanilla extract in a blender and blend until thoroughly combined and smooth.
2. Divide between glasses and top with whipped cream and cherries.
3. Enjoy!

Cookie Dough Milkshake

Forgo the cookies and milk for this AMAZING cookie dough milkshake that is completely edible and scrumptious.

Makes: 6 servings

Prep: 15 mins

Ingredients:

For the Cookie Dough:

- 9 tbsp (126g) unsalted butter, softened
- ¾ + 3 tbsp cups brown sugar
- 3 tbsp white sugar
- 3 tbsp milk
- 1 ½ tbsp water
- ¾ vanilla extract
- 1 ½ cups + 1 ½ tbsp. flour
- ¼ + 1/8 tsp salt
- 1/2 cup semi-sweet chocolate chips

For the milkshake:

- 4 1/2 cups vanilla ice cream
- 3 cups whole milk
- Whipped cream, for topping
- Mini chocolate chips, for topping

Directions:

For the Cookie Dough:

1. In a large bowl, combine the butter with the sugars and the salt using a hand mixer. Add in the milk and vanilla extract. Slowly add in the flour and mix until just combined. If the mixture is too dry, add in the water. Fold in the chocolate chips.

For the Milkshake:

1. Place the vanilla ice cream, milk and cookie dough in a blender and blend until combined and smooth.
2. Divide between glasses and top with whipped cream and mini cookies.
3. Enjoy!

Oreo Milkshake with Chocolate Ganache

A classic flavor in its own right, this milkshake takes the flavors of Oreo to the next level with the addition of a rich and luscious chocolate ganache.

Makes: 6 servings

Prep: 15 mins

Ingredients:

For the Ganache:

- ½ cup heavy cream
- ¾ cup semi-sweet chocolate chips

For the Milkshake:

- 4 1/2 cups vanilla ice cream
- 3 cups whole milk
- 24 Oreo Cookies
- ¼ cup semi-sweet chocolate chips
- Whipped Cream, for topping
- Mini Oreos, for topping

Directions:

For the Ganache:

1. Place the heavy cream in a medium-sized bowl and microwave for about 30 seconds or until cream just starts to boil. Quickly add in the chocolate chips and whisk until smooth and no lumps remain. Heat for a few seconds more if needed. Set aside to cool slightly.

For the Milkshake:

1. Place vanilla ice cream, whole milk, Oreo cookies and chocolate chips in a blender and blend until smooth.
2. Divide between glasses and top each with a tablespoon of ganache, whipped cream and mini Oreos.
3. Enjoy!

Apple and Cinnamon Milkshake

Experience the flavors of fall all-year-round with this cinnamon-spiced apple milkshake that tastes just like apple pie!

Makes: 6 servings

Prep: 10 mins

Ingredients:

- 4 1/2 cups vanilla ice cream
- 3 cups whole milk
- 1 ½ tsp vanilla extract
- 3 apples, peeled, cored and chopped
- 4 tsp ground cinnamon
- Pinch of nutmeg

Directions:

1. Place vanilla ice cream, milk, vanilla extract, apples, cinnamon and nutmeg in a blender and blend until well combined and smooth.
2. Divide between glasses and serve with a sprinkle of cinnamon.
3. Enjoy!

Coffee Milkshake

The perfect drink to get you going in the summer (or any other season really), this coffee milkshake is rich, favorful and oh-so-creamy.

Makes: 6 servings

Prep: 10 mins

Ingredients:

For the Ganache (optional but recommended):

- ½ cup heavy cream
- 6 tbsp. semi-sweet chocolate chips
- For the Milkshake:
- 5 cups cold-brewed coffee
- 4 1/2 cups vanilla ice cream
- 3 cups whole milk
- Whipped cream, for topping

Directions:

For the Ganache:

1. Place the heavy cream in a medium-sized bowl and microwave for about 30 seconds or until cream just starts to boil. Quickly add in the chocolate chips and whisk until smooth and no lumps remain. Heat for a few seconds more if needed. Set aside to cool slightly.

For the Milkshake:

1. Place vanilla coffee, ice cream, milk and ganache in a blender and blend until smooth and creamy.
2. Divide between glasses and top with whipped cream.
3. Enjoy!

Banana Milkshake

Save those ripened bananas and make this delicious, thick and creamy banana milkshake that tastes like a dream!

Makes: 6 servings

Prep: 10 mins

Ingredients:

- 3 medium-large ripe bananas
- 3 ½ cups whole milk
- 1 cup ice cream (optional)
- 7-8 ice cubes

Dircctions:

1. Place bananas, milk, ice cream (if using) and ice cubes in a blender and blend until smooth.
2. Divide between glasses.
3. Enjoy!

Chocolate Peanut Butter Milkshake

Chocolate and peanut butter (match made in heaven) come together to create this rich and creamy milkshake that is irresistibly amazing!

Makes: 6 servings

Prep: 10 mins

Ingredients:

- 2 cups vanilla ice cream
- 2 cups chocolate ice cream
- 3 cups whole milk
- 1 cup creamy peanut butter
- ¼ cup chocolate syrup
- Whipped cream, for topping
- Chocolate shavings, for topping

Directions:

1. Place vanilla ice cream, chocolate ice cream, milk, peanut butter and chocolate syrup in a blender and blend until smooth.
2. Divide between glasses and top with whipped cream and chocolate shavings.
3. Enjoy!

Cinnamon Roll Milkshakes

Super creamy and delicious milkshakes that taste just like a cinnamon roll!

Makes: 6 servings

Prep: 10 mins

Ingredients:

- 4 1/2 cups vanilla ice cream
- 3 cups whole milk
- 3 tsp ground cinnamon
- ½ cup marshmallow fluff
- Whipped cream, for topping
- Ground cinnamon, for topping

Directions:

1. Place vanilla ice cream, milk, cinnamon and marshmallow fluff in a blender and blend until well combined and smooth.
2. Divide between glasses and top with whipped cream and a sprinkle of cinnamon.
3. Enjoy!

Classic Chocolate Milkshake

A classic chocolate milkshake with an extra chocolatey twist!

Makes: 6 servings

Prep:

Ingredients:

For the Ganache:

- ½ cup heavy cream
- ¾ cup semi-sweet chocolate chips

For the Milkshake:

- 4 1/2 cups chocolate ice cream
- 1 ½ cups whole milk
- 1 ½ cups chocolate milk
- Whipped cream, for topping
- Chocolate sprinkles or shavings, for topping

Directions:

For the Ganache:

1. Place the heavy cream in a medium-sized bowl and microwave for about 30 seconds or until cream just starts to boil. Quickly add in the chocolate chips and whisk until smooth and no lumps remain. Heat for a few seconds more if needed. Set aside to cool slightly.

For the Milkshake:

1. Place chocolate ice cream, whole milk, chocolate milk and ganache in a blender and blend until chocolatey and smooth.
2. Divide between glasses and top with whipped cream and chocolate sprinkles or shavings.
3. Enjoy!

Pumpkin Spice Milkshake

Anyone who says milkshakes are only for summers has clearly never tried these heavenly and silky pumpkin spice milkshakes that taste just like fall!

Makes: 6 servings

Prep: 10 mins

Ingredients:

- 4 1/2 cups vanilla ice cream
- 3 cups whole milk
- 2 cups pumpkin purée, store-bought or homemade
- 3/4 cup packed brown sugar
- 3/4 tsp nutmeg
- 3/4 tsp ground ginger
- 1 1/2 tsp ground cinnamon
- Whipped cream, for topping
- Caramel sauce, for topping

Directions:

1. Place vanilla ice cream, milk, pumpkin puree, brown sugar, nutmeg, ginger and cinnamon in a blender and blend until smooth and silky.
2. Divide between glasses and top with whipped cream and a drizzle of caramel sauce.
3. Enjoy!

Vanilla Chai Milkshake

Warm chai flavor in a super creamy milkshake form. What more can you possibly ask for?

Makes: 6 servings

Prep: 10 mins

Ingredients:

- 3 cups whole milk
- 3 tsp ground ginger
- 12 black chai tea bags
- 3 4-inch cinnamon sticks
- 1 ½ tsp vanilla extract
- 4 1/2 cups vanilla ice cream
- Whipped cream, for topping
- Ground cinnamon, for topping

Directions:

1. In a medium-sized saucepan, combine the milk, ginger, tea bags and cinnamon sticks. Heat over medium-high heat for about 6 minutes. Remove from heat and let steep for about 10 minutes. Remove tea bags and cinnamon sticks and let cool to room temperature.
2. Place ice cream, vanilla extract and chai mixture in a blender and blend until smooth.
3. Divide between glasses and top with cream and a drizzle of cinnamon.
4. Enjoy!

Strawberry Milkshake

A thick, creamy strawberry milkshake that is the perfect cure for a hot summer day.

Makes: 6 servings

Prep:

Ingredients:

- 4 1/2 cups vanilla ice cream
- 3 cups whole milk
- 1 ½ tsp vanilla extract
- ¾ lb. strawberries, fresh or frozen
- Whipped cream, for topping
- Fresh strawberries, for topping

Directions:

1. Place vanilla ice cream, milk, strawberries and vanilla in a blender and blend until smooth and creamy.
2. Divide between glasses and top with cream and strawberries.
3. Enjoy!

Pina Colada Milkshake

Rich coconut ice cream blended with fresh pineapple and thick coconut cream brings the flavors of the Caribbean right to you.

Makes: 6 servings

Prep: 10 mins

Ingredients:

- 4 1/2 cups coconut ice cream
- 2 ½ cups coconut milk
- ½ cup cream of coconut
- ½ cup pineapple juice
- 1 cup fresh pineapple, diced
- Whipped cream, for topping
- Pineapple slices, for topping
- Coconut flakes, for topping

Directions:

1. Place coconut ice cream, coconut milk, cream of coconut, pineapple juice and fresh pineapple in a blender and blend until smooth.
2. Divide between glasses and top with whipped cream, pineapple slices and coconut flakes.
3. Enjoy!

Nutella Milkshake

No milkshake book can be complete without a Nutella milkshake and this book is no exception! Hazelnut chocolate spread in cold milkshake form, honestly what more do you need?

Makes: 6 servings

Prep: 10 mins

Ingredients:

- 3 1/2 cups vanilla ice cream
- 1 cup chocolate ice cream
- 3 cups whole milk
- 1 cup hazelnut wafers
- Whipped cream, for topping
- Crushed hazelnut wafers, for topping

Directions:

1. Place vanilla ice cream, chocolate ice cream, milk and hazelnut wafers in a blender and blend until smooth.
2. Divide between glasses and top with whipped cream and crushed hazelnut wafers.
3. Enjoy!

Salted Caramel Milkshake

A delightful combination of sweet and salty caramel milkshake that tastes like melted toffee in your mouth. And who doesn't want that?

Makes: 6 servings

Prep: 25 mins

Ingredients:

For the Caramel Sauce:

- 2 tbsp water
- ½ cup white sugar
- 1/3 cup heavy cream
- 1 ½ tbsp. unsalted butter, cut into squares
- ½ tsp vanilla extract
- ½ tsp sea salt

For the Milkshake:

- 4 1/2 cups vanilla ice cream
- 3 cups whole milk
- 1 ½ tsp vanilla extract
- Whipped cream, for topping
- Sea salt, for topping

Directions:

1. Place sugar and water in a medium-sized saucepan over medium-high heat. Stir the mixture constantly until it just starts to boil. Stop stirring and increase the heat to high. When the mixture turns into a nice amber color (5-10 minutes), remove from heat and slowly add in the cream, whisking constantly. Add in the butter and whisk again. Add in the vanilla and salt and whisk until combined.
2. Allow to cool to room temperature.
3. Place vanilla ice cream, milk, vanilla extract and caramel sauce in a blender and blend until smooth.
4. Divide between glasses and top with whipped cream and a pinch of sea salt.
5. Enjoy!

Blueberry Milkshake

The color here alone is reason to give this creamy and light milkshake a try.

Makes: 6 servings

Prep: 10 mins

Ingredients:

- 4 1/2 cups vanilla ice cream
- 3 cups whole milk
- 1 ½ tsp vanilla extract
- 3 cups blueberries, fresh or frozen
- 2 tbsp honey or maple syrup (optional)
- Whipped cream, for topping
- Fresh blueberries, for topping

Directions:

1. Place vanilla ice cream, milk, vanilla extract, blueberries and honey in a blender and blend until smooth and creamy.
2. Divide between glasses and top with whipped cream and blueberries.
3. Enjoy!

Biscoff Milkshake

A heavenly cookie butter milkshake that'll have everybody drooling.

Makes: 6 servings

Prep: 10 mins

Ingredients:

- 4 1/2 cups vanilla ice cream
- 3 cups whole milk
- 1 ½ cups biscoff spread
- 4 biscoff cookies
- Whipped cream, for topping
- Cinnamon, for topping
- 2 biscoff cookies, crushed, for topping

Directions:

1. Place vanilla ice cream, milk and biscoff spread in a blender and blend until smooth. Add in the biscoff cookies and pulse a few times or until roughly mixed through.
2. Divide between glasses and top with whipping cream, a sprinkle of cinnamon and crushed biscoff cookies.
3. Enjoy!

Key Lime Pie Milkshakes

An easy-as-pie blend of vanilla ice cream, key lime juice and graham crackers that is super creamy and delicious.

Makes: 6 servings

Prep: 10 mins

Ingredients:

- 4 1/2 cups vanilla ice cream
- 3 cups whole milk
- ¾ cup graham cracker crumbs plus extra for topping
- 2 tbsp condensed milk
- 6 tbsp key lime juice

Directions:

1. Place vanilla ice cream, milk, graham cracker crumbs, condensed milk and key lime juice in a blender and blend until smooth and creamy.
2. Divide between glasses and top with whipped cream and graham cracker crumbs.
3. Enjoy!

KitKat Milkshake

Enjoy the crunch and chocolatey flavor of KitKat with this cold, creamy and crackly milkshake.

Makes: 6 servings

Prep: 10 mins

Ingredients:

- 3 1/2 cups vanilla ice cream
- 1 cup chocolate ice cream
- 3 cups whole milk
- 16 KitKat fingers
- ¼ cup chocolate syrup
- Whipped cream, for topping
- 6 KitKat fingers, for topping

Directions:

1. Place vanilla ice cream, chocolate ice cream, milk and chocolate syrup in a blender and blend until smooth. Add in KitKat fingers and pulse a few times or until roughly mixed through.
2. Divide between glasses and top with whipped cream and KitKat fingers.
3. Enjoy!

Mango and Passionfruit Milkshake

A tropical blend of mango, passionfruit and vanilla ice cream will have you feeling refreshed in no time!

Makes: 6 servings

Prep: 10 mins

Ingredients:

- 2 1/2 cups vanilla ice cream
- 2 cups mango ice cream
- 3 cups whole milk
- ½ cup mango chunks, fresh or frozen
- Pulp of 8 passion fruits
- Whipped cream, for topping

Directions:

1. Place vanilla ice cream, mango ice cream, milk, mango chunks and passionfruit pulp in a blender and blend until smooth.
2. Divide between glasses and top with whipped cream.
3. Enjoy!

White Chocolate Mocha Milkshake

The rich mocha flavor perfectly balances out the sweetness of the white chocolate ganache in this delectable frosty milkshake.

Makes: 6 servings

Prep: 15 mins

Ingredients:

For the Ganache:

- ½ cup heavy cream
- ¾ cup white chocolate chips

For the Milkshake:

- 4 1/2 cups coffee ice cream
- 3 cups whole milk
- Whipped cream, for topping
- Chocolate covered coffee beans, for topping

Directions:

For the Ganache:

1. Place the heavy cream in a medium-sized bowl and microwave for about 30 seconds or until cream just starts to boil. Quickly add in the chocolate chips and whisk until smooth and no lumps remain. Heat for a few seconds more if needed. Set aside to cool slightly.

For the Milkshake:

1. Place coffee ice cream, milk and white chocolate ganache in a blender and blend until smooth and creamy.
2. Divide between glasses and top with whipped cream and chocolate covered coffee beans.
3. Enjoy!

Matcha Green Tea Milkshake

Trendy Matcha powder gets a cold and creamy makeover with this delicious and light milkshake recipe.

Makes: 6 servings

Prep: 10 mins

Ingredients:

- 4 ½ cups vanilla ice cream
- 3 cups whole milk
- 3 tbsp high quality matcha powder plus extra for topping
- Whipped cream, for topping

Directions:

1. Place vanilla ice cream, milk and matcha powder in a blender and blend until smooth and creamy.
2. Divide between glasses and top with cream and matcha powder.
3. Enjoy!

Cannoli Milkshake

Orange, cinnamon and ricotta come together to create a creamy twist on the Italian pastry.

Makes: 6 servings

Prep: 10 mins

Ingredients:

- 4 1/2 cups vanilla ice cream
- 3 cups whole milk
- 1 ½ tsp vanilla extract
- 3 cups ricotta cheese
- 2 tbsp semi-sweet chocolate chips
- 3 tsp orange zest plus extra for topping
- 1 ½ ground cinnamon
- Whipped cream, for topping

Directions:

1. Place vanilla ice cream, milk, ricotta cheese, chocolate chips, orange zest and cinnamon in a blender and blend until smooth.
2. Divide between glasses and top with whipped cream and orange zest.
3. Enjoy!

Coconut Almond Milkshake

A silky smooth coconut almond shake that's rich and flavorful while being light at the same time.

Makes: 6 servings

Prep: 10 mins

Ingredients:

- 3 ½ cups vanilla ice cream
- 1 cup coconut ice cream
- 3 cups almond milk
- 6 tbsp unsweetened coconut flakes plus extra for topping
- ¼ cup almond butter
- Whipped cream, for topping
- Slivered almonds, for topping

Directions:

1. Place vanilla ice cream, coconut ice cream, almond milk, coconut flakes and almond butter in a blender until smooth.
2. Divide between glasses and top with whipped cream, coconut flakes and slivered almonds.
3. Enjoy!

Red Velvet Milkshake

This one's for all those red velvet cake lovers out there! Creamy, thick and delicious, this recipe is everything a good milkshake should be.

Makes: 6 servings

Prep: 10 mins

Ingredients:

- 4 ½ cups chocolate ice cream
- 3 cups whole milk plus more as needed
- 1 cup red velvet cake mix
- Whipped cream, for topping
- Chocolate shavings, for topping

Directions:

1. Place chocolate ice cream, milk and red velvet cake mix in a blender and blend until smooth and creamy. Add a bit more milk if the milkshake is too thick.
2. Divide between glasses and top with whipped cream and chocolate shavings.
3. Enjoy!

Tiramisu Milkshakes

A glass of this thick, creamy and drool-worthy milkshake will satisfy any coffee-lover out there.

Makes: 6 servings

Prep: 10 mins

Ingredients:

- 4 ½ cups vanilla ice cream
- 1 cup whole milk
- 1 ½ tsp vanilla extract
- 2 cups espresso coffee
- ½ cup mascarpone cheese
- ¼ cup heavy cream
- 6 ladyfinger biscuits
- Whipped cream, for topping
- Cocoa powder, for topping

Directions:

1. Place vanilla ice cream, coffee, milk, mascarpone cheese, heavy cream and ladyfinger biscuits in a blender and blend until smooth and creamy.
2. Divide between glasses and top with cream and a dusting of cocoa powder.
3. Enjoy!

White Chocolate Raspberry Milkshake

Smooth and luscious white chocolate ganache mixed with fresh raspberries make for a delicious milkshake recipe.

Makes: 6 servings

Prep: 10 mins

Ingredients:

For the Ganache:

- ½ cup heavy cream
- ¾ cup white chocolate chips

For the Milkshake:

- 4 ½ cups vanilla ice cream
- 3 cups whole milk
- 3/4 lb. raspberries, fresh or frozen
- Whipped cream, for topping
- Fresh raspberries, for topping

Directions:

For the Ganache:

1. Place the heavy cream in a medium-sized bowl and microwave for about 30 seconds or until cream just starts to boil. Quickly add in the chocolate chips and whisk until smooth and no lumps remain. Heat for a few seconds more if needed. Set aside to cool slightly.

For the Milkshake:

1. Place vanilla ice cream, milk, white chocolate ganache and raspberries in a blender and blend until smooth.
2. Divide between glasses and top with whipped cream and raspberries.
3. Enjoy!

Dark Chocolate Brownie Milkshake

Dark chocolate lovers rejoice! This ultra-creamy, dark chocolate milkshake contains pieces of dark chocolate brownie making this the ultimate dark chocolate milkshake.

Makes: 6 servings

Prep: 40 mins

Ingredients:

For the Brownies:

- 1/4 cup unsalted butter
- 1/4 cup dark chocolate chips
- 1/2 cup white sugar
- 1 large egg
- 1 tsp vanilla extract
- 1/4 tsp salt
- 1/4 cup unsweetened cocoa powder
- 1/4 cup all-purpose flour

For the Milkshake:

- 2 ½ cups vanilla ice cream
- 2 cups chocolate ice cream
- 1 ½ tsp vanilla extract
- 3 cups whole milk
- Whipped cream, for topping
- Chocolate shavings, for topping

Directions:

For the Brownies:

1. Preheat the oven to 350°F/175°C. Line a 9X5 inch pan with baking paper and set aside.
2. Place butter and chocolate chips in a heat-proof bowl and microwave in 20 second intervals until melted. Add in the sugar and mix until well combined. Add in the egg and vanilla extract followed by the salt, cocoa powder and flour and mix until just combined.
3. Pour batter into pan and bake for about 25 minutes. Remove and set aside to cool.

For the Milkshake:

1. Place vanilla ice cream, chocolate ice cream, milk and brownies in a blender and blend until smooth.
2. Divide between glasses and top with whipped cream and chocolate shavings.
3. Enjoy!

Peach Pie Milkshake

Cinnamon-spiced peach milkshakes with brown sugar and vanilla ice cream makes this milkshake the perfect pie-like treat for summer.

Makes: 6 servings

Prep: 10 mins

Ingredients:

- 4 ½ cups vanilla ice cream
- 3 cups whole milk
- 6-7 medium-large ripe peaches, chopped
- 6 tbsp brown sugar
- 1 ½ tsp ground cinnamon plus extra for topping.
- Whipped cream, for topping

Directions:

1. Place vanilla ice cream, peaches, milk, brown sugar and cinnamon in a blender and blend until smooth.
2. Divide between glasses and top with cream and a dash of cinnamon.
3. Enjoy!

Cotton Candy Milkshake

Embrace your inner-child with this fun and delicious cotton candy milkshake that'll make everyone go on a little sugar high.

Makes: 6 servings

Prep: 10 mins

Ingredients:

- 4 ½ cups vanilla ice cream (Can substitute with 3 cups vanilla ice cream + 1 ½ cups cotton candy ice cream)
- 3 cups whole milk
- 1 ½ cups blue or pink cotton candy plus extra for topping
- 1 ½ tsp vanilla extract
- Whipped cream, for topping
- Sprinkles, for topping

Directions:

1. Place ice cream, milk, cotton candy and vanilla extract in a blender and blend until smooth.
2. Divide between glasses and top with whipped cream, cotton candy and sprinkles.
3. Enjoy!

Conclusion

Well, there you have it! You've reached the end of this recipe book that contains some of the best milkshake recipes ever. Go ahead and try each and every one of them and make sure to save some for your friends and family!

About the Author

Born in New Germantown, Pennsylvania, Stephanie Sharp received a Masters degree from Penn State in English Literature. Driven by her passion to create culinary masterpieces, she applied and was accepted to The International Culinary School of the Art Institute where she excelled in French cuisine. She has married her cooking skills with an aptitude for business by opening her own small cooking school where she teaches students of all ages.

Stephanie's talents extend to being an author as well and she has written over 400 e-books on the art of cooking and baking that include her most popular recipes.

Sharp has been fortunate enough to raise a family near her hometown in Pennsylvania where she, her husband and children live in a beautiful rustic house on an extensive piece of land. Her other passion is taking care of the furry members of her family which include 3 cats, 2 dogs and a potbelly pig named Wilbur.

Watch for more amazing books by Stephanie Sharp coming out in the next few months.

Author's Afterthoughts

I am truly grateful to you for taking the time to read my book. I cherish all of my readers! Thanks ever so much to each of my cherished readers for investing the time to read this book!

With so many options available to you, your choice to buy my book is an honour, so my heartfelt thanks at reading it from beginning to end!

I value your feedback, so please take a moment to submit an honest and open review on Amazon so I can get valuable insight into my readers' opinions and others can benefit from your experience.

Thank you for taking the time to review!

Stephanie Sharp

For announcements about new releases, please follow my author page on Amazon.com!

(Look for the Follow Bottom under the photo)

You can find that at:

https://www.amazon.com/author/stephanie-sharp

*or Scan **QR-code** below.*

Printed in Great Britain
by Amazon

45982856R00047